MONKEY MOVEMENT

MONKEY MOVEMENT

THE ULTIMATE GUIDE FOR MONKEY KUNG FU
MOVEMENTS, TECHNIQUES, AND ACTING

SIFU BRIAN KUTTEL

Copyright © 2020 by Brian Kuttel
All rights reserved. This book or any portion thereof
may not be reproduced or used in any manner whatsoever
without the express written permission of the publisher
except for the use of brief quotations in a book review.

Printed in the United States of America

First Printing, 2020

ISBN 978-1-7352946-0-5

"Do not seek to follow in the footsteps of the masters. Seek what they sought."

Matsuo Basho

Table of Contents

Monkey Movement   1

Monkey Movement   3

Introduction   1

Choy Li Fut History   3

How to Use This Book   6

Choy Li Fut Monkey Form Description   8

Monkey Walk	10
Monkey Cross Step	12
Monkey Run	14
Barrel Roll	16
Forward Roll	18
Somersault	20
Backward Roll	22
Headstand	24
Handstand	26
Cartwheel	28
Roundoff	30
Back Tuck	32
Rolling Back Fall	34
Back Fall	36
Handspring	38
Headspring	40
Kip up (Pop up/kick up)	42
Scissor Sweep	44
Leg Flower	46
Forward Sweep	48
Grinding Wheel Sweep	50

Back Sweep	52
Ground Side Kick	54
Ground Back Kick	56
Front Kick	58
Monkey Slap	60
Backhand Slap	62
Thrusting Palm	64
Rising Palm	66
Finger Jab	67
Monkey Acting	68
Monkey Posture	69
Eating and Chewing	70
Finding and Eating a Flea	70
Eating a peach	71
Shading the Eyes	72
Blinking	73
Fidgeting	73
Scratching	73
Washing face	74
Monkey Expressions while Walking	74
Final Thoughts	75
About the Author	77

MONKEY MOVEMENT

Introduction

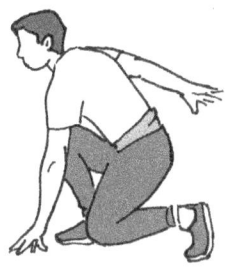 

The inspiration of this book comes from the Monkey form of Choy Li Fut kung fu, however it is not necessary to know Choy Li Fut, let alone any kung fu style to benefit from this book. In fact, this book is a guide for movement training, not form instruction, and not for fighting applications. The various techniques will help you better explore your own potential in the realm of physical movement. Whether or not you are planning to use these movements for martial purposes, training will have a positive effect on your strength, balance, coordination and all around athleticism. If you know the Choy Li Fut monkey form, or a monkey form from another style, this book will serve as a great reference when refining your technique. If you are looking to broaden your range of movement, dig in, there's a lot of information ahead.

I have trained for twenty years in the art of Choy Li Fut kung fu and have known the Monkey form for almost half of that time. I learned it direct from my Sifu, Jason Wong, son of world renowned Grandmaster Doc-Fai Wong. Sifu Wong has a very strict eye for detail and sets very high standards when it comes to martial arts, something I take pride in as his student because he has given me more depth and breadth in my understanding and abilities in the martial arts. I have since kept the form active in my practice routine, and notice the benefits all around in the rest of my martial arts when the monkey form is sharp.

In terms of Choy Li Fut, the way I view the monkey style, as with other of the kung fu animals, is that it cannot function solely by itself and be considered a "well-rounded" standalone system. The techniques can be valuable for specific conditions in fighting, but are not able to adapt to the majority if not all conditions as an established art. I prefer to think of animal styles as add-ons, or upgrades to a base art. Like a Swiss Army knife of martial arts, when you need the tool it's there. There is no need for exclusivity when it lowers the amount of movements available in any given situation.

However, there is a time and a place for everything, so if the conditions are just right, a couple of monkey slaps, a rolling kick and some following acrobatics would make for a very entertaining fight. However, realistically the chances of that happening are very slim and to blindly approach a fight with "looking cool" in mind will not likely end well for you. Instead, take the monkey movements and form as a challenge of training, to be able to do things that most cannot do, and then the strength and abilities you've acquired through training will improve your fighting ability.

Have fun and happy training!

Sifu Brian Kuttel

MONKEY MOVEMENT

Choy Li Fut History

Choy Li Fut kung fu is one of the most popular styles of Southern kung fu. Developed in 1836 by a man named Chan Heung. It comprises the lessons of his lifetime of training under three different martial artists and kung fu styles. With low southern style stances and many different hand striking positions, coupled with high northern style kicks and dynamic combinations, Choy Li Fut is as beautiful to watch as it is a devastating fighting style. There are over 200 forms or choreographed routines lasting from 50 to as much as 300 movements, ranging from hand forms, to weapon forms, two-person combat hand and weapon forms, internal forms and even three-person fighting forms. A student of Choy Li Fut is not expected to know all 200 forms to be deemed a master, and in fact proficiency of the art can be achieved with knowledge of about 30 forms. The incredible amount of forms in just one system makes for a lifelong pursuit of the art and keeps the student always learning. Some of the most unique hand forms in Choy Li Fut are among the ten animal forms taught. The ten animals of Choy Li Fut are: Tiger, Leopard, Snake, Crane, Dragon, Monkey, Lion, Tiger Cub, Horse, and Elephant. The majority of forms in the system were not created upon conception of the art, including animal forms, and thus as the art branched off into different locations and lineages which resulted in either multiple forms under the same name or subject, and are specific to that lineage.

Grandmaster Doc-Fai Wong began learning Choy Li Fut from famed Hung Sing Choy Li Fut Master, Lau Bun in San Francisco. As he progressed in the art, he began to help out and teach classes and students. When Lau Bun passed away in 1967, Doc-Fai Wong continued to teach at Hung Sing Kwoon until moving out to open another location in Chinatown. Eventually, he moved out of Chinatown and into the Sunset District of San Francisco where his school currently resides today. After a few years of teaching on his own, he sought out to continue his Choy Li Fut training which took him to across the ocean to Hong Kong in search of a new teacher. Eventually, he not only found one but two well-known Choy Li Fut masters who not only agreed to teach him but accept him as a direct disciple simultaneously, which in martial arts culture and tradition of strictly only having one Sifu, is almost unheard of. However, both Hu Yuen Chou and Wong Gong agreed together, to make him a closed-door student and performed the discipleship ceremony at the very same banquet. Grandmaster Doc-Fai Wong has since taught the three lineages of Choy Li Fut of his teachers: Hung Sing (Fut San style) Choy Li Fut from Lau Bun, King Mui (Chan Heung's village) Choy Li Fut from Hu Yuen Chou, and Jiangmen (previously called Kongchow) Choy Li Fut from Wong Gong.

MONKEY MOVEMENT

The Monkey form that has been passed down from Grandmaster Doc-Fai Wong comes from the Jiangmen lineage from Great Grandmaster Wong Gong. The monkey form is considered an advanced level form because of the difficulty level of the acrobatic movements as well as some of the movement sequencing, and until more recently was scarcely seen. For many years, only Grandmaster Doc-Fai Wong, his son Sifu Jason Wong (who also learned the set directly from Great Grandmaster Wong Gong) and a couple select disciples were the only ones who knew the form. Nowadays, the form has been passed down and taught publicly, however most students who learn the form either never complete it due to the strenuous techniques or can no longer perform the physically demanding form for other reasons. Although exposure and availability of learning is more than ever, the Monkey Form continues to remain a rare and elusive form.

Sifu Jason Wong

Brian Kuttel

How to Use This Book

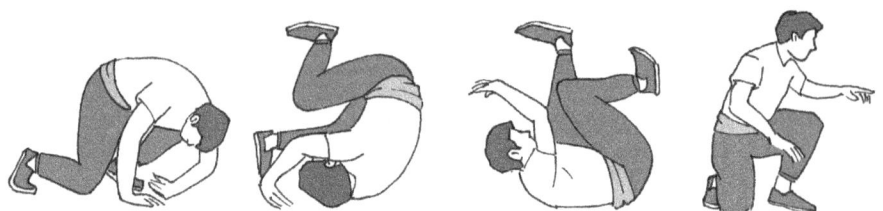

This book is intended as a reference guide and therefore can be read from any point the reader wishes to begin, and in any order. Though having a grasp of some basic techniques can facilitate an easier time in the learning of more difficult ones, the reader may choose to pick up their techniques and movements in any order. Most techniques (excluding acting) exist in other Choy Li Fut Forms so this may also provide insight into why the movements are used in a training sense. It is important to always practice in a safe environment with proper supervision, and reader assumes all risk of injury upon practice. If the reader is unsure about any technique, it is best to seek professional advice from a gymnast or capable martial artist.

It is also suggested to use this book as a base of exploration and to further the scope of possibilities by looking to resources and inspiration outside the book and art like Peking Opera, other kung fu styles, kung fu cinema, breakdancing, parkour and movement training. There are also the traditional methods of developing the monkey form by observing monkeys in nature, either by visit to a zoo, or by watching online videos.

MONKEY MOVEMENT

This book will help cover some fundamental groundwork, but the rest is to be experienced and explored in any direction the reader chooses to pursue. A key element to pick up some techniques and then learn by having fun!

*Please note that all techniques will be explained with a right hand dominant side for consistency, both sides of techniques should be learned to properly develop the body and craft. Some images have been reformatted to a left to right sequence for ease of sequence.

Brian Kuttel

Choy Li Fut Monkey Form Description

The Choy Li Fut Monkey Form is not a long form, especially when it comes to actual martial arts techniques and movements. The form is broken down into 65 total movements, over half of which is comprised of monkey acting and acrobatics, leaving about 30 movements of martial technique. The beginning of the form after the initial salute is monkey acting, as if telling a story about a monkey in its day to day activities of looking around for food, grooming and preening, and eating fleas. The monkey turns its attention to a big juicy peach and cautiously steps out into the jungle before being scared back to its tree. The urge to sink its teeth into the juicy peach is too enticing for the monkey and so again the monkey ventures out into the jungle and this time snatches up the peach to feast. As the monkey blissfully eats the sweet fruit, it is suddenly attacked!

At this point, the rest of the form kicks in to full gear and monkey acting is placed second to the fighting techniques, save for little moments after certain techniques as to not abandon the monkey aesthetic. Many of the movements involve low stances and even ground rolling and sweeping techniques, however there are single leg balancing techniques which builds a contrast of high and low as well as emphasis on different muscle groups and stabilizers. Both hand strikes and kicking techniques are dispersed between parrying and evasive footwork. The form is closed by a quick monkey running lap, and then some fancy acrobatic movements before the final salute to end the set.

MONKEY MOVEMENT

Although the set is not complicated, the constant low stances coupled with the high flying acrobatic movements are very physically demanding earning its place in the advanced level of Choy Li Fut.

Regardless of belt rank or title, the skill level of the martial artist can be identified in their performance of all three aspects of the form; their martial arts basics (stances, structure, strikes, kicks) must be strong and effective if used in combat, their gymnastic ability should be springy and appear effortless, and their monkey acting should seem natural as the animal, not an overdone caricature or halfhearted.

To possess all three of these characteristics is very rare as most practitioners tend to be strong in only one or two, but the ideal should be kept in mind when observing and in training, to aspire to the highest level.

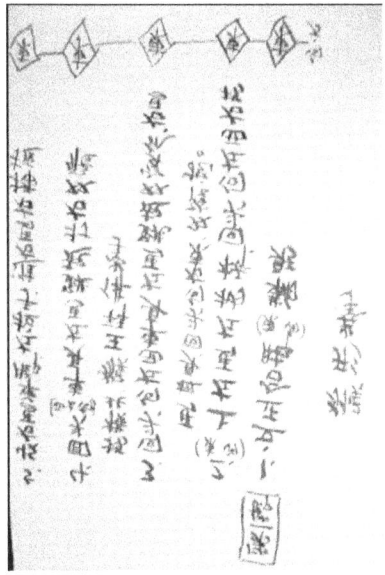

Choy Li Fut Monkey Form Script

Monkey Walk

Movement

The Monkey Walk is the cornerstone of movement of the monkey form, and is the foundational movement for strength and coordination training. The weight of the body is distributed to the hands and the feet with alternating steps of hands then feet. The typical walk moves the body sideways rather than straight forward, with the back hand crossing the front hand, and then the back foot crossing the front foot, and has a slight rocking motion as the bodyweight is shifted from hands to feet. Monkey walking keeps the body low to the ground and is an excellent exercise for coordination development as well as muscle build for the arms, legs, and core simultaneously.

Method

From a standing position, crouch as low as possible by bending the knees without sitting down, the heels may lift off the ground as needed. Hunch slightly forward and place the palms on the ground, between the knees, keeping the majority of your bodyweight on the feet. Take the left hand and reach to the right, crossing in front of the right arm and place it on the ground. Lift the right palm off the ground and move it to the right, reaching past the left hand, and place it on the ground. Shift the bodyweight to the hands to allow the feet to move easily. The left foot will cross in front of the right foot as it travels to the right and finally the right foot will step past the right hand, ending with the body in the same position as it started. This action of left hand, right hand, left foot, right foot, is considered one monkey step and can be simply repeated to continue the monkey walk.

Mistakes

The most common mistake in performing the monkey step is not shifting enough bodyweight to the hands and simply placing them on the ground. This will affect the timing of the step and instead of having four different components, will become one hop. The best way to practice the correct timing and weight shift is to slow the movement down into a four count, and emphasize leaning forward to put more weight on the hands.

The monkey walk should be practiced at all speeds, not only for the sake of the form, but for total movement training development. The slower the movements, the more muscles will work to stabilize and control the movement. It may not seem like an incredibly complicated movement, but it can do so much for the body. Monkey walking should always be practiced at varying speeds before every single monkey kung fu training session.

Monkey Cross Step

Movement

The Monkey Cross Step is a type of monkey walking for moving diagonally. However, instead of the four-count timing of the hands and feet of the monkey walk, the monkey cross step is accomplished by placing the hand and foot down at the same time, creating a two-count timing.

Method

From a standing position, step forward with the left foot and bend the knees until reaching a lunging position making sure to keep the right knee off the ground, and touch the right hand to the ground, with the left monkey hand behind. Cross step with the right foot diagonally forward and to the left, touching the left hand to the ground next to the right foot. Step with the left foot diagonally forward to the left, replacing the left hand as it raises up and back, touch the right hand down to the ground in front of the body. The step can continue depending on how far you want to traverse and can be practiced at multiple speeds either fluidly or with pausing on each step.

MONKEY MOVEMENT

Mistakes

The most common mistake in performing the monkey cross step is raising the stance too high, and rushing the movement. The best way to prevent this mistake is to emphasize touching the hands to the ground and to practice pausing in each position.

Monkey Run

Movement

The Monkey Run is similar to leaping and vaulting in parkour, the movement is a straight forward jump to plant the hands on the ground and gaining extra distance with the feet. The hands and feet move together in pairs and alternate. Ideally, the hands and feet do not touch the ground at the same time. There are variations in directions of travel in relation to body position, sometimes sideways moving like a faster version of the monkey walk, but most times is performed moving straight ahead.

Method

From a standing position, crouch down to the ground as low as possible, the heels may lift off the ground as needed. Swing the arms forward and upward as you press with the feet and jump forward and upward. It is important to reach forward as if diving, leveling the body in midair. Touch down with the hands, arms still extended, and allow the hips to swing forward and bring the feet forward outside of the arms. Lift the hands to allow the feet to touch down and prepare for the next leap. The priority of the leap is to move more forward than upward.

MONKEY MOVEMENT

Mistakes

The most common mistake in the monkey run is to not alternate the timing of the feet and hands and simply leap and land on all fours simultaneously. The best training to eliminate this habit is to simply break the run down into two steps, leap to the hands, then land the feet, then stop and reset. Eventually connecting the running steps together will become seamless.

Variations

There are variations to the monkey run depending on the strength and flexibility of the practitioner. If the arms are strong enough and the legs are flexible, the legs can shoot through between the hands to gain even further distance which is more like a parkour vault. Running laps in the monkey run will greatly develop the strength and stamina of the practitioner and can be a standalone workout for the arms, legs, and core.

Barrel Roll

Movement

The Barrel Roll is performed during the monkey run to add some uniqueness and playfulness to the run by jumping up into the air and rolling sideways and then landing back in the monkey running position. The rotation of the barrel roll is 360 degrees, and difficulty is dependent on the feet getting higher off the ground in respect to the level of the upper body.

Method

From a crouching position with hands and feet on the ground, swing the extended left arm upward and back over the body, simultaneously raise the left leg upward in the same direction. As the body begins to turn to the left, push with both the right hand and foot to propel the body upward as it continues the rotation. At the height of the jump, the back will be towards the ground and the arms and legs (knees still bent for monkey style) extended outward and upward. The rotation will continue in midair until the hands and feet return to their original orientation and land on the ground. The barrel roll can be completed in the same spot, or traveling in the direction of the roll. It is best to practice both methods to develop a strong understanding of this technique.

MONKEY MOVEMENT

Mistakes

The most common mistake for the barrel roll is disconnection of the arms and legs from the torso which will result in an off balance or improperly timed movement. This can be due to the practitioner trying to think things through in in separate steps. The movement is fast and is completed by momentum so it cannot be stifled by thought process.

Forward Roll

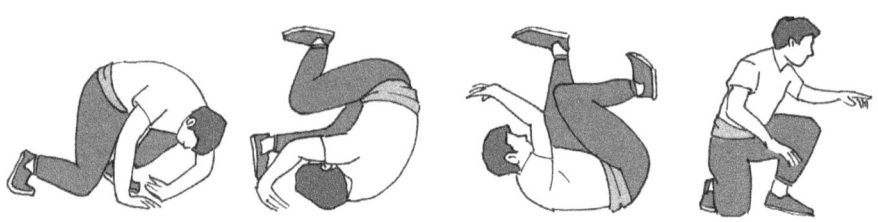

Movement

The Forward roll is a forward shoulder roll in which ground contact of the spine is minimal and is the not only the safest, but most efficient way to roll forward. The path of the roll will start from one shoulder and continue to the opposite side hip as if drawing a diagonal line across the practitioners back. The forward roll is not only a method of moving, but is also a safety net for when things go wrong in other acrobatic movements and a recovery from loss of balance or fall is needed.

Method

From a standing position take one step forward with the right foot and then lower the left knee to the ground like a lunge, making sure to keep the angle of both bent legs 90 degrees and not sitting on the heel. Round the back as you hunch forward and tuck your chin into your left armpit. Keep the elbow of the right arm bent so that the arm is rounded and extend the right hand back, along the ground, next the left knee. Keeping your right shoulder to the inside of your right knee, lean forward until the right shoulder touches the ground. Maintain the rounded posture and curved back and let the forward momentum carry your feet over your head. There are many ways to conclude the roll, however the most practical is to keep the left leg tucked, allowing the right foot to be planted firmly on the ground upon arrival in a position of which you may simply stand from.

MONKEY MOVEMENT

Mistakes

When rolling accurately and successfully from a kneeling position becomes consistent, you can start from a standing position, then stepping forward and instantly rolling. When stepping into a roll can be accomplished with ease, then practice by placing an object in front of your feet and then rolling over it without making contact to the object. Later you can add momentum and jump or dive into a forward roll. It is best to take the time to perfect the forward roll with both left and right shoulders as they are both utilized in the monkey form.

Somersault

Movement

The Somersault, is a forward rolling technique in which the emphasis is central and not on a particular side or shoulder. It is important to practice proper form as this roll directly contacts the length of the spine along the intended path on the ground. The body must remain rounded so there will not be excessive pressure on any part of the back. The somersault can also be a safe exit or in worst case scenario a safety net for aborted handstands and headstands.

Method

From a standing position, feet hips distance apart (or more if necessary) squat down evenly to the ground. Tuck the chin down to the chest and round the back as you lean forward. Extend the hands out to guide the body (do not try to stop momentum as it could result in injury to the wrists and hands). As the body leans forward, keep the chin tucked as you will avoid head contact and first contact the ground touching your shoulders. Maintain a rounded posture as until the roll is completed and you arrive with the feet planting on the ground.

MONKEY MOVEMENT

As efficiency is reached, you can begin by a low hop into the somersault, like a forward tuck or low front flip into the roll, often called a "peanut roll." It is always important to practice this roll on a soft surface until you have complete confidence in your ability to perform the technique.

Backward Roll

Movement

The backward roll is as it states, rolling backward from a front facing direction, sending the feet over the head to either returning to a standing position, or laying flat out as seen in some of the acting techniques. Mastery of this technique goes beyond performance as the body is highly vulnerable to injury from a fall backward. Being able to roll backward and distribute the impact of the fall will not only help you avoid, but protect yourself against injury. Because the feet move together over one particular shoulder, it is recommended to practice the roll on both right and left sides.

Method

From a standing position, squat as low as possible (heels up or down does not matter). Tuck the chin straight down and round the back. Sit down and lean back, maintaining the rounded posture and let momentum carry the bent legs over your head. Once the feet have passed the line of the shoulders, extend them straight back in the direction of the roll, both together over the right shoulder. Once the feet reach the ground, follow the momentum and return to a standing position, using the hands if necessary. The arms can be held in a number of positions during the backward roll, most commonly extended with palms down to either side upon reaching the ground, but it is suggested in the beginning of learning the roll to keep the arms in until the roll is completed as extending the arms out may slow or stop the momentum of the roll which can hinder your progression.

Once the basics can be performed efficiently, you can start from a standing position and then sinking to the ground by sliding a foot forward, toes turned out, to let the entire side of the extended leg contact the ground (like the rocking bar on a rocking chair) until reaching the hip to the ground to begin the backward roll. Make sure to practice not dropping straight to the ground as this could result in injury to the tailbone. An excellent indicator of proficiency for any rolling technique is the sound of the roll, the quieter the roll, the better the technique.

Headstand

Movement

The Headstand is completed by balancing on the crown of the head and hands on the ground with legs extending upward. Though it is an excellent exercise by itself, it is also a suggested pre-requisite for the handstand in which the arms are fully extended and the head does not touch the ground.

Method

From a seated kneeling position with both knees on the ground, place the hands shoulder distance apart on the ground with the fingers pointing forward. Lean forward and touch the crown of the head to the ground, a common mistake is to touch the forehead which will put a tremendous amount of pressure on the neck once the legs are lifted off the ground. The shape of the head and hands touching the ground should make a triangle, and an easy way to tell is if you can see your hands in your peripheral vision. It is a common mistake to place the hands in line with the head which will provide no extra support for the headstand, and although a balanced position is achievable it is much more difficult. Once the proper triangular alignment is achieved, the next step is to walk the feet in towards the body until the knees can rest atop the bent elbows and the pelvis is raised directly above the shoulders. Once the knees are on the elbows, evenly shift the weight off the toes to the knees letting the feet lift up off the ground. Keeping the knees bent at a 90-degree angle and using the hips as an axis of rotation, bring the legs up until the soles of the feet point upward and the body appears as if in an upside down sitting position. Next, keeping the feet and knees together, extend the feet upward until the legs are at full extension completing the headstand.

It is good training to pause at each position before moving to the next, and is important to perform each movement slowly to maintain proper balance. If you lose balance and fall towards your back, round the back and roll like a somersault which will prevent a flat landing straight on the back. Exiting the headstand can be done by either bringing the feet down to their starting position by hinging at the hip, or by simply rolling out of it like a somersault.

Handstand

Movement

The Handstand is performed by balancing the body upside down on only the hands. The palms are flat on the ground, the arms extended downward to support the rest of the body upward.

Method

From a standing position, extend both arms out in front of you with hands shoulder distance apart. Take a lunging step forward with the right foot, and bending at the waist and keeping the head and eyes looking at your hands, place the hands on the ground. As the body leans forward lift your left leg, making sure to keep it straight and toes pointing, until the toes point straight up. Let your left leg momentum pull your right leg up into the air as you shift your weight completely over the hands. Bring the feet together, clenching the knees together. It is important to maintain structure the entire time and keeping all necessary muscles engaged. Do not bend the elbows as it will put more weight on the biceps and shoulder muscles which are not usually capable of holding bodyweight for very long. Instead, keep the elbows locked out to allow the bones to hold weight. Exiting a handstand can be done by lowering the feet back down along the path they came up, or rolling out with a forward somersault, or letting the knees bend and legs extend over the head making a bridge once they reach the ground, then standing back up to complete a walkover.

Hand Stands are not an easy technique and require much assisted practice to give the body time to learn how to support bodyweight on the hands and balance it once it is up. Handstands against a wall are a great way to practice in the absence of a partner to assist and hold your legs. Walking in a handstand can also help develop the supporting muscles needed for a strong handstand.

Cartwheel

Movement

The cartwheel is a fundamental gymnastic technique which puts the structure of the handstand into motion. It can be the gateway to further techniques such as the roundoff, one handed cart wheel, and even an aerial (cartwheel without hands). It is performed with arms and legs extended outward, like spokes of a wheel, as the body rolls forward from hand to hand to feet again. The cartwheel is also used as a way to generate momentum for more advanced techniques that need an extra push before initiating.

Method

From a standing position, take a long step forward like a lunge with the right foot and extend the arms up into the air, engaging the shoulders and keeping the arms locked out and straight on either side of the head next to the ears. Keeping the torso facing forward, bend forward at the waist until it is parallel with the ground, raise the left leg until it is also parallel with the ground. Bend further forward and place the right hand with the fingers turned out to the right in line in front of the toes. The left leg will continue to raise until pointing directly upward as you place the left hand, with fingers pointing in the same direction as the right hand, shoulder distance apart. At this point both hands will be in line and the fingers pointing in the same direction, the arms will still be locked out and next to the ears. Simply straighten the right leg to push it forward and follow the left leg over the top. As the left foot touches down, firmly plant the foot and raise the hands up similar to the starting position, the right leg will arrive last and the body should be in a left lunge position.

Mistakes

It is important for martial artists to consciously keep their elbows locked out as it can be counter intuitive to their training. It is also important that the legs and lower body remain directly above the torso to keep balance and proper technique. Lastly, be sure to extend the legs, even pointing the toes, throughout the duration of the cartwheel. If you are having balance issues, practice your handstands help correct any posture or structure.

Roundoff

Movement

In appearance, the roundoff is similar to a cartwheel in which the hands are placed on the ground and the extended legs pass overhead, however the feet are met together at the midpoint, straight up, directly above the body and are then turned inward toward the direction of origin and land together. Timing of the hands on the ground will differ slightly, but the biggest change in technique is that there is some punch force in the arms to build more of a springing action. Because the feet are brought together, more collective weight can mean more momentum and potential energy which can facilitate a much more energy intensive technique like a back handspring or back tuck (backflip).

Method

From a standing position, take a long step forward like a lunge with the right foot and extend the arms directly up next to the head. Bend forward, keeping the arms next to the ears and the torso pointing forward, raising the extended left leg upward. Place the right hand in line with the right foot with the fingers pointing toward the right, then the left hand in line with the right at shoulders distance apart and fingers pointing in the same direction. Quickly raise the right leg to meet the left leg at the apex and as the weight shifts onto the hands, a quick burst of extending energy in the arms will spring the feet more upward and as they continue in the forward motion the body will raise up off the ground slightly before landing with the feet together pointing in the direction of origin. It is common to release the created energy of the movement by a hop before finishing the landing, or the momentum can be used directly to power the next technique.

Mistakes

As with the cartwheel, one of the most common mistakes is leaving the hands on the ground too long, disconnecting the core and losing power. Another common mistake it to bend the elbows too much which directly destabilizes the arms and puts all the bodyweight on the biceps to support. Practicing handstands will develop the fundamental structure that is to be maintained throughout the movement of the roundoff and correct any positional mistakes.

Back Tuck

Movement

The Back tuck is also known as a backflip and one of the most impressive acrobatic techniques in the Monkey Form. In the traditional Choy Li Fut Monkey form script, it actually calls for three consecutive backflips in a row, which is no easy feat, especially considering they are at the very end of the set, after the legs have been fatigued with low monkey stances. The back tuck is performed with an upward jump, bringing the feet over the head in a backward rotation in midair and then landing again on the ground. The back tuck is not a simple technique and requires much practice and due to the high risk of injury, should not be attempted or practiced, without proper safety equipment and proper supervision.

Method

Starting from a standing position, squat down extending your arms downward and back until they are behind you. With force, swing the arms forward and upward, push hard with the feet to propel yourself straight up into the air. Tilt back slightly to direct your momentum and at the height of the jump, tuck the arms and knees in to allow full rotation, then extend the feet out to land with knees bent to absorb the energy of the technique.

Mistakes

One of the most common mistakes in attempting a back tuck is to throw the head backward, which will flatten out the body in midair stopping the rotation and landing on the neck or the back. Another of the more common mistakes is to not jump upward or high enough to allow full rotation. The key to the back tuck is in the spring and leg power of the jump, therefore squat jumps can be a tremendous help in developing your back tuck. If you have a spotter to help your technique, they should not have to work much to guide you over. If they are lifting or straining to help your technique, you need to go back to practice and build more leg strength as you are not ready to be spotted.

Rolling Back Fall

Movement

The rolling back fall is a backward roll which is stopped once the shoulders reach the ground, not allowing the feet to pass over the head. It is done as a way to stop momentum from an out of control roll, or as a safe way to land a fall when thrown. The rolling back fall is an excellent way to develop proper positioning for falling as well as condition the body to take falls from varying heights.

Method

From a standing position, feet shoulders distance apart, squat down as low as possible (heels may come up off the ground) and arms crossed at the chest with the hands open. Keep the back rounded, tuck the chin towards the chest, and tilt backward letting gravity begin your roll. The moment your upper back between the shoulders (trapezius muscles) makes contact to the ground, extend the arms out, palms down and slap the ground making contact only with the palms. Keep the legs tucked in for the entire duration of the fall, as well as the tucked chin. The slap does not need to be hard, you are not fighting the ground, but releasing momentum and extending the platform of contact, like a tripod, to stabilize the body.

MONKEY MOVEMENT

Never use the arms to prop out and stop the momentum of the fall, that will quickly result in injury to the shoulders, elbows, and wrists. It is also important to not hit your elbows to the ground when slapping out to the sides. There are different schools of thought when it comes to proper angle to extend the arms, whether directly out to the sides or with a downward angle (near the hips). As long as the palms are not next to the body, and the arms do not pass above the line of the shoulders, anywhere in that range is safe and can be left up to your own personal preference as which to use.

Mistakes

The most common mistakes are not maintaining a rolled-up or rounded position and landing flat on the back. Another very common mistake is to let the head tilt back and hit the ground. Both can be resolved by practicing backward rolls, or by sitting and rocking back and forth, from shoulders to glutes, hugging the knees in to the chest.

Back Fall

Movement

The back fall is exactly as it sounds, and can be done from various heights depending the skill of the practitioner to safely land on their back after throwing themselves upward and backward into the air, landing with their back on the ground.

Method

From a standing position with feet shoulders distance apart, squat down as low as possible and cross the arms in front of the chest with hands open. Keep the chin tucked as you arch your back and fall back to your shoulders without touching your head to the ground. The hips will raise and the heels may come off the ground as if making a bridge position. The arms will extend outward and can slap as in the rolling back fall, but as height is increased, the arms will extend out and act like antennae to 'find' the ground and guide the body to the correct position. The arms must not be propped with elbows locked out to stop the fall as that will result in injury to the wrists, elbows, and shoulders. Because you cannot see the ground and the level of responsiveness for the hands is acute, this is a dangerous technique to perform, so take your time in increasing height to the preliminary jump. As height is increased, the legs can be used to diffuse the momentum of the fall, bending at the hips and throwing the momentum out through the feet putting less pressure on the back and shoulders.

Mistakes

Most common mistakes are from misguided falls, landing on the head or neck directly, or lower on the spine or back. These can easily be trained away by practicing backward rolls and rolling back falls. Another prominent mistake is to extend the arms out to stop the fall rather than guide the body, which will result in injury to wrists, elbows, and shoulders in the least. A final mistake that is common is in the jump, which must be upward, as jumping outward extends the back instead of maintaining the rounded position which will lead to landing flat on the back. Practicing from a lower height and on soft surfaces under proper supervision will help keep you safe in practice.

Handspring

Movement

The Handspring is a technique in which the hands are brought forward quickly to the ground and the feet are propelled forward over the head springing off the hands, much like a front flip with the legs extended, but with the hands touching the ground to power the technique.

Method

From a standing position, take a step forward with your right foot and bend your knee, like a lunge while raising the arms up and next to your head. Place your hands down directly in front of your foot, arms straight with the shoulders engaged, and hands shoulders distance apart. Bring both legs up above the body to an inverted position like a handstand but without stopping the forward momentum. As the feet reach directly above the body thrust with the arms down to spring up off the ground. The legs will pull the upper body back to right side up as they return to the ground.

The key to the handspring is momentum, and a strong press with the hands on the ground. An easy way to begin this technique to take a couple steps forward to build momentum before throwing the palms down and 'punching' off the ground. The legs should swing over rather than bending the knees to kick outward for power as the spring itself comes from the hands. There are variations of handsprings depending on the timing of the feet, if traveling together, or consecutively which is commonly referred to as a "walkover."

Mistakes

The most common mistake is bending the elbows before pressing off the ground, for more power, which actually reduces the structure and stability of the position. Another common mistake is bending the legs too much in rotation, you want a strong momentum to pull you over which comes from extension of the legs. Similarly, letting the legs extend laterally from the center will not only throw off your balance, but will consequently lose momentum. To develop proper position and structure for the front handspring it is recommended to practice hands stands, and work on a springy surface floor.

Headspring

Movement

The headspring is similar to the handspring in which the legs are thrown forward over the body and back to a standing position, however the defining element to the headspring is that only the crown of the head makes contact to the ground. In fact, the headspring is closer to the pop up in technique and could be considered a pop up from a headstand. There's no assistance form the hands and the arms are often folded behind the back, however in the beginning stages, it is suggested to place the hands on the ground to help guide the head down without unintentionally striking the head.

Method

From a square horse stance position with arms folded comfortably behind the back, sink into the stance to lower the torso as much as possible as it will make the head contact lighter and safer. Lean forward with the upper body until the crown of the head is on the ground, extend the legs to bring the hips over the head and follow the momentum as if doing a headstand. Bend the knees again as the torso aligns, because the only way to generate force to raise the body off the ground will come from the feet kicking up and out. Once the feet pass above the head kick upward and forward to throw the body off the ground. Engage the core as if doing a fast sit up and as the feet return to the ground the upper body will return to a natural upright position. Again, hands may be used to balance the head on the ground and can push following the legs kicking to help complete the technique, however the ideal position is with the arms folded comfortably behind the back. Flexibility can be helpful in the ease of this technique, so it is suggested that you are able to comfortably bend forward from a straddle position and touch the head to the ground without raising the heels.

Mistakes

The most common mistake is moving too slow, hindering the necessary forward momentum which will end in falling straight on your back. Another common mistake is not kicking hard enough, or in the correct direction. Kicking out too soon will only make the body hop upward, when the trajectory needs to be both upward and forward. Conversely, kicking out too late will only flatten the body resulting in landing flat on the back.

It is important to have a strong neck and back for this technique as you will be concentrating your bodyweight over the neck, and the forward swinging and kicking motion may have an effect on the back. Practicing headstands and pop ups will make the headspring a much easier technique to learn.

Kip up (Pop up/kick up)

Movement

The kip up is an impressive method of springing up onto the feet from a starting position of laying on the ground. The kip up is performed by rolling back to the shoulders and tucking the legs in and then kicking up and outward to bring the practitioner up off the ground and to their feet. There are many variations involving the hands for assistance or without the hands, as well as knees bent or legs fully extended, and finally degrees of landing position in relation to starting position (180, 360).

Method

From a standing position, squat down until seated, keeping the knees bent upward and back rounded as if preparing for a backward roll. Roll back to the shoulders and place the hands on the ground as close as possible to the shoulders, allowing the hips to raise up, keeping the knees bent and chambered at the chest. Kick upward and outward with the heels to initiate the lift, then immediately extend the arms to assist the raising of the body. Pull the body upward like a sit up to help carry the torso up and over the feet as they land on the ground to a standing position.

Another variation is to keep the legs extended and rather than kicking straight out, swing the legs forward to generate power to lift the body off the ground. Hands are helpful to assist, but not necessary. Other variations require the body to rotate while in mid-air so that upon landing, face the opposite direction, or even make a full 360-degree rotation before landing.

Mistakes

The most common mistake in the kip up is the direction of the kick, either straight up, or not angled enough and straight out, both will lead to an unsuccessful technique. Another common mistake in regards to the kick is not consolidating the energy of the legs and kicking out in multiple directions, or by letting the legs recoil, both of which absorb the generated momentum which is necessary to complete the technique.

A soft surface is always suggested, but not required in learning the technique, as it usually takes many failed attempts landing on the back before a successful kip up. Practicing on an incline or elevated platform will also help the body get used to coordinating in mid-air which will help refine the technique for flat surfaces.

Scissor Sweep

Movement

The scissor sweep is a martial technique that uses the legs like scissors to swing sideways in opposite directions to forcefully trip an opponent. There are varying methods of application mostly depending on the height of attack. A jumping scissors sweep will attack the lower torso, or hips, and knees. The more common lower attack can be done from the ground, attacking the knees and ankles. In the monkey form, the martial artist is propelled forward off their hands to directly attack the legs for a low scissor sweep. In forms, it is commonly followed by a Leg Flower to stand up again.

Method

From a standing position with the right foot forward, squat down as low as possible without sitting on the ground. Reach forward with both hands, passing the inside of the right knee, and place both palms on the ground simultaneously. Leap forward off the feet, staying low, propping yourself on the arms and kick both feet forward with the hips sideways and the right leg on top. Cross the extended legs as far as possible with the right leg to the left side, and left leg to the right side. Keep the hands in contact with the ground to aid a softer landing on the left hip (you can slightly rotate the hips to allow landing on the balls of the feet and make more points of contact, however it should be subtle and not affect or stall your technique). As soon as the hip touches the ground, immediately swing your extended legs back to the opposite side, scissoring and attacking your opponent's knees with your right hamstring and calf and their ankles with your left shin, forcing them to trip over your left leg and effectively taking them down to the ground. It is important to note that this can work with your opponent facing either direction, but is more common that you attack behind the knees and in front of the ankle.

Mistakes

The most common mistake in application is not getting enough leverage by only using the leg from the knee down. This happens when the practitioner does not shoot in far enough and executes the technique too soon. When you shoot in for the takedown cross your legs as much as possible and use the upper leg (above the knee) to push on their closest leg with as much leverage as possible.

Leg Flower

Movement

The Leg Flower can be used either to obstruct a standing opponent while on the ground, or to use momentum to bring one to their feet, or even in martial application as a sweeping technique. It involves swinging the legs in a circular motion while on the ground to generate enough force to lift the upper body in the direction of motion.

Method

From a lying position with your back on the ground. Tilt to the left hip and prop the torso up with the left elbow and both hands on the left side of the body with the legs extended and spread, left leg to the left side and right leg to the right side. Begin by swinging the right leg towards the left, like a roundhouse kick, as the right leg passes the left tilt back and lie down circling the extended leg around in the same motion, bringing your knee as close as you can to your chest much like an outside crescent kick. The left leg will follow the right leg and pass over the body much like an inside crescent kick. As the left leg passes the torso, let the momentum pull you up towards your right, tucking your right leg under the left, bringing you to a kneeling position where you can stand up. This should be done quickly and all in one motion as to efficiently use the weight and motion of the legs to pull the body forward to a kneeling position.

MONKEY MOVEMENT

Variations of the leg flower mainly involve adding an upward and outward thrust with the legs like a kip up which will continue the spin like a corkscrew as it pulls you up off the ground and to your feet.

Mistakes

The most common mistake when performing the leg flower is bending the knees too much, it is important for momentum as well as appearance to keep the legs as extended as possible until reaching the other side. Bending the knees too much is a result of trying to position the legs too soon for the kneeling part, and a simple way to correct it is to focus on extension the entire time and not allow the knees to bend until both legs have passed the torso.

Forward Sweep

Movement

The forward sweep is called 'sow geuk' in Choy Li Fut ad is performed by sweeping the back foot forward in a circular motion along the ground with the leg at full extension. The forward sweep is most commonly performed with a range of 45-degrees, however some sweeps will encompass 180-degrees. The back leg is bent as much as possible to allow maximum extension of the sweeping leg, but remains solid with the heel on the ground as it is the center axis of the sweep. The hand position varies depending on the sweep, sometimes striking in the opposite direction with a back fist or open hand to complete the application, however in the Choy Li Fut Monkey form the forward sweep is performed with the hands touching the ground to keep the body as low as possible for the full 180-degree range sweep.

Method

From a standing position with left foot forward and right foot back, bend down over the left knee and extend the arms forward to place the hands on the ground, right hand in front of left on the same line, to the left side of your front foot. Keep your right leg extended as you swing it forward with the foot flat on the ground and toes pointing inward. Allow the hands to support the weight of the body as the left foot will need to pivot to the left and support the swing of the right leg around. The end position will be with the left leg bent, toes pointing to the left and heel down, hands planted firmly on the ground between the knees, and right leg extending forward with foot turned in so the toes point to the left.

Mistakes

One of the most common mistakes in performing the forward sweep is not allowing the sweeping foot to move in a large circular path, and instead bringing the foot in close to the body and then extending out in a straight path along the ground to the end position as if doing a sliding sidekick forward. The best way to train out of this habit is to practice on a smooth surface to allow contact to the floor, but with little to no friction, and by not bending all the way down. As the body gets used to swinging the leg around and forward it will become easier to lower the stance for the correct position.

Applications of most Choy Li Fut movements are usually more compact versions with higher stances than in the training movements of the forms, however, the forward sweep must be done exactly as the form to allow maximum reach for the sweeping leg to attack not just one, but both of the opponent's legs for a successful technique.

Grinding Wheel Sweep

Movement

The Grinding Wheel Sweep is one of the fancier techniques on the ground. It can be seen as a continuous front sweep without the upper body turning and is also a very popular movement in breakdancing. In application, the grinding wheel sweep is meant to develop coordination and strength, not to be used as a continuous sweep as there is not enough power generated to take an opponent down after the initial sweep.

Method

From a standing position with the right leg back, bend the left knee and extend the arms forward until the hands touch the ground, as the body drops forward, swing the right extended leg forward in a circular path just like a regular front sweep along the ground with the toes pointing forward into the sweep. However, continue the momentum of the leg without losing speed, while using the planted hands and left foot as a central axis for the sweep. As the right leg reaches the right arm, raise the hand off the ground to let the leg pass under and then replace it in its original position. As the leg reaches the left arm, lift the hand to let the leg pass under, then replace the hand to the ground once the leg has passed. At this point it is common to let the toes of the right leg point upward and is completely acceptable. As the right leg reaches the left foot, shift the bodyweight forward to the hands as if getting into a push up position and hop up with the left foot, jumping over the right leg. Keep the right leg extended and let it rotate as it continues around to the starting position, and repeat the steps to make the sweep seamless and continuous.

The most common mistake for the grinding wheel sweep is by bending the sweeping leg's knee when it reaches the left foot which usually results in wrapping and or sweeping the left foot. The key to this is to emphasize full extension of the right leg as it passes around. Another common mistake is to sprawl out and extend the left leg as it hops over the right foot landing in a more proper push up position and thus ending the sweep, this can be remedied by a constant awareness of the left leg, and keeping the knee bent even when hopping over. The last common mistake is leaning back to place the hands on the ground behind the body during the sweep. The hands must always return to the same place on the ground in front of the body and only raise to let the leg pass. If necessary, place markers on the ground for the hands to be placed during the sweep.

Though as an entire technique, the grinding wheel sweep serves no direct fighting application, the technique requires agility and balance in movement and utilizes all four limbs making for excellent movement training to develop the practitioner's strength, agility, and coordination.

Back Sweep

Movement

The back sweep is a low circular swinging kick with the posting leg bent completely and hands on the ground to allow the body to pivot and the fully extended sweeping leg maintain foot contact to the ground during the sweep. The range of sweep will vary between a typical 90 degrees to an entire 360 degrees. The calf and heel are used to strike and sweep the opponent's foot causing them to fall to the ground.

Method

From a standing position with the left foot forward and right foot back, bend both knees and turn towards the right knee, placing the palms on the ground with fingers turned as far to the right as possible. As you bend downward, keep your weight on your left leg and begin swinging the right leg, heel first, outward behind the body (clockwise for right leg) 180 degrees towards the front while keeping the foot in contact with the ground. To continue the sweep to 360 degrees, place the hands down later and add more power to the swinging leg to allow it to pull the body all the way around.

MONKEY MOVEMENT

Mistakes

One of the most common mistakes is the back sweep is separating the sinking and the swinging which results in a weak sweep. The key to completing this technique relies in momentum of the leg, so practicing higher up and turning to sweep, without placing the hands on the ground, will help you develop comfort in the motion and gradually you can sink lower and lower until the hands touch the ground. Another common mistake is the angle of the leg in relation to the body, which can be identified by the foot position. If the extended leg is in proper position out to the side of the body, the sweeping foot will remain flat on the ground with the heel leading the sweep, if the angle of the leg is more toward the front of the body, the toes will raise off the ground pointing upwards, or if the leg is too far behind the body the toes will point downwards.

Ground Side Kick

Movement

The Ground Side Kick is a thrusting kick from a laying on the ground position similar to the final position of a side fall, using the blade edge and heel of the foot to kick at the attacker's shin, knee, or rest of the body depending on their position. The ground side kick is one of the more practical techniques of the Choy Li Fut Monkey form, but should be used only when the opponent is too close to allow a recovery of footing.

Method

From a standing position with the feet together, squat down as low as possible brining the knees to the chest, rounding the back, and tucking the chin (to prevent hitting the head back on the ground). Lean back, turning slightly to the left so that only the left side of the body from hip to shoulder make contact with the ground. As the body rolls back, extend the left arm out to the side to slap the hand against the ground. Make sure not to let the elbow hit the ground before the palm, and keep the left knee bent and leg tucked under to protect the groin while kicking. Kick by thrusting the right foot out with the toes turned sideways to the left, striking the opponent with the blade edge of the foot (from the pinky toe to the heel) but mostly on the heel as it is better supported by the leg. The right hand may also be placed as support on the left side of the body next to the left hand during the kick. As with any kick, it is important to return the leg back to the knee bent chambered position before moving to another stance or technique.

Mistakes

The most common mistake in performing the ground side kick is an incorrect position of the body, with both hips on the ground which will directly affect the power and alignment of the kick. The hip of the kicking leg should not be on the ground at all and the torso should only make contact on the side from hip to shoulder. An excellent indicator of hip position is by looking at the direction of the toes when kicking, if the toes tend to turn upward, the body is not turned sideways enough.

In the Choy Li Fut Monkey form, the ground kick is usually performed out of a forward shoulder roll. A good way of knowing which leg to kick with is dependent on which shoulder is used to roll, therefore a right shoulder roll results in a right ground side kick. The timing is simple, as the roll is near completion turn slightly to the side and slap outward with the left hand, also letting the torso unravel out of its rounded position to stop the forward rolling momentum as the kick is released using extra momentum from the roll to increase striking power.

Ground Back Kick

Movement

The Ground Back Kick is a thrusting side kick utilizing the bottom of the foot and heel in a stomping motion to kick the opponent's shins, knees, stomach, lower ribs, and solar plexus. Unlike the ground side kick, the ground back kick is thrown from a position of the hands and knees on the ground. The all fours position allows for a faster recovery to standing after kicking and supports more power in the kick by the hand position which braces the body for a solid landing kick. Being higher off the ground also allows the practitioner to kick more targets along the opponent's legs, upwards to the torso, and even the head depending on the situation.

Method

From an all fours position, with the hands and knees on the ground and back flattened, looking over the right shoulder. Raise the right leg outward to the right, keeping the knee bent at 90 degrees, until the hip, knee, and foot are level on the right side of the body chambering the kick. Kick by thrusting the heel directly back (towards the opponent), keeping the foot turned so the toes point to the side like a side kick. As with any kick, it is important to bring the leg back to the chambered position before moving to another stance or technique.

Mistakes

The most common mistake in throwing a ground side kick is trying to kick too high which sacrifices proper technique and will not allow the leg to be fully extended. Full extension is imperative to landing a solid kick as it allows all momentum and energy to travel through the leg into the intended target. Any bend can cause disconnect and noticeably reduce the power and effect of the kick. To remedy this, practice lower kicks and pausing once the leg is at full extension. Flexibility and strength will improve through consistent practice.

Front Kick

Movement

The front kick is a quintessential martial arts technique found in nearly every style of martial arts. There are slight stylistic differences for the monkey front kick that tend to only change the look of the kick but do not change the effectiveness. It is typical in the Choy Li Fut form to pair the front kick with a simultaneous hand strike like a thrusting palm or finger jab, which is completely optional in general practice outside the form.

Method

From a cat stance with the right foot forward and monkey hands in a ready position guarding the body, bring the right knee up in a bent position to chamber the kick in front of the chest. Aesthetically, the toes of the foot point forward, which is against what is commonly taught of keeping the toes pointing down, as the forward toes increase the monkey appearance. Thrust the foot forward with the toes curled upward, extending the leg fully, striking with the ball of the foot. Retract the leg to the bent knee position before returning it to the ground. Various foot positions can be used depending on the intended target, ranging from toes pointing forward using the instep of the foot to kick upward to the groin, hands, or chin; to using the ball of the foot or the heel to kick the face, throat, sternum, solar plexus, or ribs. Just as hand strikes can be practiced from various stances, so should kicks as well as using front leg and back leg for kicking proficiency.

Mistakes

The most common mistake is to swing the leg upward for the front kick to gain height or extend the leg faster. The kick should be a forward thrust resulting from a hinging action of the bent leg. The best way to remedy the upward swing is to practice pausing in the chambered position with the kicking leg raised, and knee bent, before kicking.

Monkey Slap

Movement

The Monkey Slap is a large sweeping slapping strike with the palm of the hand. In the Choy Li Fut Monkey form, the monkey fist hand position is a relaxed cupped palm, with no overly fancy finger articulations. It is important to unify the hand when slapping to not let loose fingers snap other fingers on the hand which could cause self-injury.

Method

From a cat stance position with the left foot forward and right foot back, Monkey hands in a ready position guarding the body, step forward with the left foot to a sideways horse stance position, drop the right hand out to the side with the palm facing forward. Turn left to a bow stance and use the hip to drive the torso, whipping the relaxed palm forward, to deliver a horizontal slap to the face. Maximum effect will come from using the heel of the palm to strike with knockout power, but more surface area in the slap will cause more pain to the opponent.

It is important to keep relaxed throughout the slap, as it is intended to cause pain to an opponent by striking the ear, temple, jaw, or even along the ribs and exposed arms.

MONKEY MOVEMENT

There is a variation of the monkey slap in which the striking path is vertical instead of the horizontal path explained above. Beyond the difference of path, the mechanics of the movement are essentially the same. Stances can also vary from lower kneeling stances to twisting stances so it is important to take time and explore how to facilitate the strike from various positions.

Backhand Slap

Movement

The backhand slap is another signature strike in the Choy Li Fut Monkey Form. Instead of a horizontal outward slap (or reverse slap), the backhand slap is actually a forward thrusting strike with the knuckles along the back of the hand. Although the motion can generate a substantial amount of power and deliver a painful sting, it will not deliver a knockout strike. That is why it is typically used to stun an opponent to set up for other more devastating strikes.

Method

From a cat stance position with the right foot forward and monkey hands in a ready position guarding the body. Quickly thrust the left hand forward with the fingers together, held horizontally and the palm facing in toward the body, keeping the arm relaxed allowing the back of the hand snap and strike once at full extension. Immediately retract the left hand back, moving under the right, as the right hand thrusts the backhand slap forward. This should land like a typical boxing 1,2 succession, fast and with snapping power.

MONKEY MOVEMENT

In a training sense, the backhand slap is one of the most beneficial movement training techniques in the monkey form, developing relaxed power and speed which will translate over into all of the practitioner's striking techniques. An excellent way to train this technique is to throw combinations of increasing amounts of consecutive backhand slaps, with the striking hand moving up and over the returning hand, similar to chain punching in Wing Chun. Start from combinations of two strikes, then work upward in odd numbers (three, five, seven…) to allow alternation of initiating strikes. As with all hand strikes, stances will vary from lower kneeling stances to twisting stances so it is important to take time and explore how to facilitate the strike from various stance positions.

Thrusting Palm

Movement

The trusting palm is a direct, straight-line strike utilizing the heel of the palm as a striking surface which delivers much more of a solid blow compared to the sweeping monkey slap. It can be considered the hand equivalent to the side kick, in both position and power transfer.

Method

From a cat stance position with the right foot forward and left foot back, monkey hands in a ready position guarding the body, bring the right palm up to the shoulder with the fingers pointing to the left. Step forward with the right foot to a sideways horse stance positon and thrust the palm directly forward, keeping the fingers pointing to the left and striking with the heel of the palm. The momentum of the forward step coupled with the thrusting power of the arm will create a strong linear force that can cause much damage if properly landed.

MONKEY MOVEMENT

Relaxation is always important to begin with to allow a much faster strike; however, the palm and body must tense up just before to moment of impact to yield the most power. Such palm strikes harbor more devastating effects and can be used to target the nose, temples, chin, jaw, clavicles, solar plexus, sternum and ribs. As with all hand strikes, stances will vary from lower kneeling stances to twisting stances so it is important to take time and explore how to facilitate the strike from various positions.

Rising Palm

Movement

The rising palm is an open handed thrusting uppercut. The heel of the palm is used as the striking surface targeting the throat, jaw, nose, sternum, solar plexus and ribs. The main discerning difference between the rising palm and thrusting palm is the direction of the fingers. The thrusting palm has the fingers pointing inward, whereas the rising palm has the fingers pointing outward.

Method

From a cat stance position with the right leg forward, monkey hands in ready position, step forward with the right foot to a sideways horse stance position and drive the right palm forward and upward with the fingers turned out towards the right, striking with the heel of the palm. Much like other straight-line strikes, power comes from body momentum and thrusting of the arm. The striking surface is the heel of the palm as it has the most driving force behind it. As with all hand strikes, stances will vary from lower kneeling stances to twisting stances so it is important to take time and explore how to facilitate the strike from various positions.

Finger Jab

Movement

The Finger Jab is an outward forward flick with the finger tips usually to either damage the eyes, temporarily blinding the opponent, or to distract the opponent from a simultaneous, or following technique. Not to be mistaken for a thrusting or eye gouging technique, the finger jab is a flicking, tapping motion that should not sacrifice speed for power.

Method

From a cat stance position with the right foot forward, monkey hands in a ready position guarding the body. With a hinging motion of the elbow, quickly extend the hand forward so that the fingers can tap the opponent's eyes. Keep the fingers extended, but relaxed and not held tightly together so that they can work around obstacles on the face like the brow or nose and find their way into the eyes. This should be done in an unraveling and snapping motion, quickly retracting as fast as striking out. As with all hand strikes, stances will vary from lower kneeling stances to twisting stances so it is important to take time and explore how to facilitate the strike from various positions.

Monkey Acting

Monkey acting is a key element in performing any monkey kung fu regardless of style. The spontaneous and erratic movements will instantly reveal that the performance is of the monkey and thus engages the audience into the antics on display. Without the primate idiosyncrasies, the form would just be like any other kung fu form with an added handful of acrobatics, and although that can be seen as a spectacle of itself, the monkey is iconic in kung fu culture and a skilled portrayal of the animal coupled with expert technique commands respect of not only the audience but other practitioners.

Even if performance is not the goal of learning the monkey form, the acting is a part of the heritage and history of the style, and a tradition that must be perpetuated through practice of acting as serious as practice of the rest of the form. Herein lies the double edge sword of monkey form practice, because if either the acting or the martial techniques are inferior, or superior to each other, the lack will be what is seen and remembered; if the monkey acting is good, but the martial techniques are bad, the practitioner will look weak and silly; if the techniques and skills of the form look strong and crisp, but the monkey acting is lacking, it looks awkward and disconnected. Thus, for the serious practitioner, consistent practice of both on an equal level is suggested.

MONKEY MOVEMENT

Monkey Posture

The largest physical change for the martial artist is in assuming a monkey posture to mimic the body and movement of the monkey. Simple adjustments like rounding the back and raising the shoulders, tucking the elbows close to the body and, quick erratic movements can make the performer appear to be more monkeylike.

Monkey Face

The face is one of the most important elements of monkey acting and can vary depending on the style, form, and practitioner's personal style. The basics are large attentive eyes, constantly looking around for food or predators. In Chinese Opera, there is an emphasis on bursts of quick, non-stop blinking, and in other kung fu styles the eyes can also be used to convey emotion of whether the monkey is frustrated or inquisitive. The mouth is usually manipulated, by either pulling the chin downward to stretch the upper lip over the length of the upper teeth, even sometimes (though not the safest during acrobatic movement) the tongue is placed between the front teeth and upper lip to exaggerate the lips and give a more monkey like appearance. An exaggerated chewing motion with the mouth closed is also done from time to time to give more movement to the mouth and face. Sometimes, the nose is used to show the monkey smelling by either flaring the nostrils or scrunching the nose.

Eating and Chewing

A simple way to describe eating and chewing is to exaggerate our normal human actions of taking a bite and chewing. Bringing the food to the mouth should be done like scooping water, and can be done with either one or two hands. The bite should look large, and then chewing should look exaggerated, all while looking around for more food or predators. Random hesitations or pauses before returning back to eating can show the monkeys short attention span.

Finding and Eating a Flea

Finding the flea is usually performed after scratching the knee. Naturally a monkey would simply eat the bug, but in acting can be broken down into three phases; catching, plucking, and eating. Catching starts with normal scratching that is interrupted by the monkey noticing the tasty flea, the monkey then poises itself and swiftly catches the flea. Holding it up by the index finger and thumb to get a better look, the monkey then uses the other hand and plucks the wings off the flea, one at a time, with quick and accurate jerks. The monkey then quickly tosses the flea into its mouth and then chews and enjoys its snack.

MONKEY MOVEMENT

Eating a peach

Eating a peach is a bit different than when the monkey eats a flea or small snack, the peach is a big prize and a big meal for the monkey. Discovery of the peach should be highlighted in acting, and even as the monkey approaches, it should appear excited and even greedy as it snatches it into its clutches. The monkey holds the peach with two cupped hands, and takes very large bites from the fruit, then looks up and around, even over the shoulder, to make sure no one is around to steal the peach. When the monkey is done, both hands are used to throw out the pit, allowing the monkey to continue.

Shading the Eyes

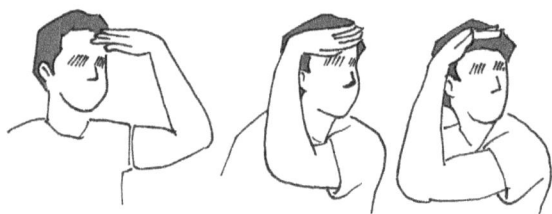

Shading the eyes is a signature characteristic of kung fu and Chinese Opera Monkey forms. It can be used to show the monkey searching for food, or to emphasize a posture or pause during a form. There are three ways to shade the eyes, the first is to simply raise the hand up to the brow naturally, palm down, with the index finger at the forehead. Because it is how a human would shade their eyes, other monkey facial expressions should be used to maintain the monkey appearance. The second variation is a much more distinct expression with the hand again being placed upon the brow, but with the elbow turned across the body, palm down, and pinky at the forehead. The position of the arm across the body and hand turned all the way around is very unique and will stand out to the audience. The third variation is much like the second but with one slight adjustment, again turning the elbow across the body, but rather than palm down, the palm will be up the thumb at the forehead shading the eyes with the back of the hand.

Blinking

Blinking is not a necessary technique for kung fu forms, but is highly emphasized in Chinese Opera. Monkey blinking is accomplished by rapid successive blinking with wide open eyes, many of these blinking bursts last from 30-50 blinks in a matter of 5 seconds which can be a very difficult feat to perform. Blinking should be coupled with other monkey acting techniques to truly embody the animal.

Fidgeting

Simple quick, sharp, instantaneous movements of looking around, scratching, or simple hops give a more active monkey appearance but should not be done back-to-back in succession otherwise the appearance will become robotic and awkward. Fidgeting can be performed to emphasize other acting techniques but should not be done to overshadow the other technique.

Scratching

Scratching is a standard when it comes to monkey acting techniques and there are several typical locations that are scratched in the Choy Li Fut monkey form; the belly, chest, armpits, knees, and behind the ears. Both hands are used to scratch the belly, including the ribs alongside, additionally one can stop in place while the other hand continues to give a more realistic effect. The armpits are scratched using the hand of the same arm, reaching across to scratch the opposite armpit tends to look too natural for a human and will appear out of place. knees and quadriceps can be scratched while in either a squatting or kneeling position with either both hands simultaneously or just with one hand. Lastly, to scratch behind the ears, the monkey hand is raised up behind the ear with the palm forward as the body hunches slightly forward to help the hand reach. Scratching should be fast and vigorous and used to show that the monkey is comfortable enough to divert its attention from food or predators.

Washing face

Washing the face or grooming is typical in many styles of monkey acting but is not commonly seen in the Choy Li Fut monkey form. To wash the face, the hands are brought across to the opposite side of the body and then over the head as if brushing the hair or fur. Washing can be done in either direction and can even have the hand travel more around the head horizontally than the typical diagonal or vertical directions. Washing is best done in a short burst of about four to six passes with the hands.

Monkey Expressions while Walking

While monkey walking, it is important to use monkey acting to both keep the appearance of a monkey, but in the case of the Choy Li Fut form, to maintain the story. Little additions to walking around like tapping the hand on the ground, or chewing, or even quick turns to look can reveal what is enticing the monkey to maneuver to a particular spot, or why it is running away.

Final Thoughts

The Monkey form is a unique treasure in the Choy Li Fut system. It preserves a legacy of theatrics and stories from ancient times and as well develops the physical strength and coordination to create a stronger, faster, more adaptable fighter. The true benefit for combat comes from movement training, not from acting. To think that one can act like a monkey during a real serious fight is naïve and delusional. Any experienced martial artist knows to never underestimate an opponent, and only when there is a complete obvious difference in skill level can one use the monkey acting in conjunction with monkey fighting to "outclass" their opponent. However, that case is rare and should not be the goal of training, rather it should be to improve oneself in all manners of mobility, to challenge oneself to become stronger, faster, more agile… more mobile.

If you have been lucky enough to learn the monkey form, you have been given a gift, an heirloom from the past masters. Regardless of your goals in training, take all elements of the form and practice them seriously. Practice the acting as much as you practice the acrobatics and fighting techniques. Preserve the tradition so that you may continue the legacy by one day passing it down to the next generation as pure as you learned it.

Even if the form has not been learned, practice of the individual monkey techniques can be just as valuable. A simple form can be created by chaining a number of techniques together for an enjoyable practice. The key to unlocking the full potential of movement comes from the freestyle mode of training. After the form and techniques are fully comprehended and performed at an exemplary level, one needs to put away the order of movements and seek to explore movement itself in real time, just as a fighter shadowboxes, the monkey stylist can change their direction, pace, technique and movement seamlessly from one direction to the next. Then truly the ideal of monkey kung fu training can be embodied. The monkey is playful, so treat your training as play, enjoy your movements, enjoy your life!

About the Author

Sifu Brian Kuttel has been training in Choy Li Fut kung fu and Yang tai chi since 2000 and earned his black sash at Tiger Kung Fu Academy in Reno NV under the tutelage of Sifu Zai. In 2008 Brian moved to San Francisco to work full-time as Program Director at Doc-Fai Wong Martial Arts Center where he continued to progress in his skills and training with his Sihings and Sifu Jason J. Wong. In 2014 he was officially recognized with the title of Sifu by his Sifu Jason Wong and Grandmaster Doc-Fai Wong and was officially accepted through *bai si* ceremony as a direct disciple of Jason J. Wong. In 2018 Brian moved from San Francisco to where he currently resides in Geneva Switzerland, teaching classes locally, and seminars and workshops internationally.

Since 2008, Brian has promoted Choy Li Fut and Yang tai chi by creating and uploading videos to YouTube which has grown a following over the years. Under the encouragement of Grandmaster Doc-Fai Wong, Brian began writing and submitting articles to national martial arts publications and was featured in Inside Kung Fu Magazine and multiple times in Kung Fu Tai Chi Magazine. Monkey Movement is his first book, and hopefully one of many to come ranging across both Choy Li Fut kung fu and Yang tai chi.

YouTube: https://www.youtube.com/c/SifuKuttel
Patreon: https://www.patreon.com/sifukuttel
Facebook: https://www.facebook.com/kungfukuttel
Twitter: https://twitter.com/sifukuttel
Instagram: @SifuBrianKuttel
Twitter: @SifuKuttel

www.ingramcontent.com/pod-product-compliance
Lightning Source LLC
Chambersburg PA
CBHW031224090426
42740CB00007B/697